The
Thunderbirds

The Thunderbirds

George Sullivan

Illustrated with photographs

Dodd, Mead & Company • New York

Copyright © 1986 by George Sullivan
Distributed in Canada by
McClelland and Stewart Limited, Toronto
Printed in Hong Kong by South China Printing Company

2   3   4   5   6   7   8   9   10

Library of Congress Cataloging-in-Publication Data

Sullivan, George, 1927–
    The Thunderbirds.

    Includes index.
    Summary: Describes the operation of the U.S. Air Force's crack aerial demonstration squadron, the Thunderbirds, including the team's history, selection and training of pilots, and planning and executing a show.
    1. United States. Air Force. Thunderbirds—Juvenile literature. [1. United States. Air Force. Thunderbirds. 2. Stunt flying. 3. Aeronautics, Military] I. Title.
UG633.S85   1986   797.5′4′0973   86-6259
ISBN 0-396-08787-6

Acknowledgments

The author is grateful to the many people who contributed information and photographs used in this book. Special thanks are due: Captain Ron Lovas, the Thunderbirds; Major William Austin and Captain Peter Meltzer, Department of the Air Force, Washington, D.C.; Z. Joe Thornton, General Dynamics; Ira Chart, the Northrop Corporation; Captain Bob Williams and Rick McCluskey, Hanscom Air Force Base, Boston, Massachusetts; and Aime LaMontagne.

Contents

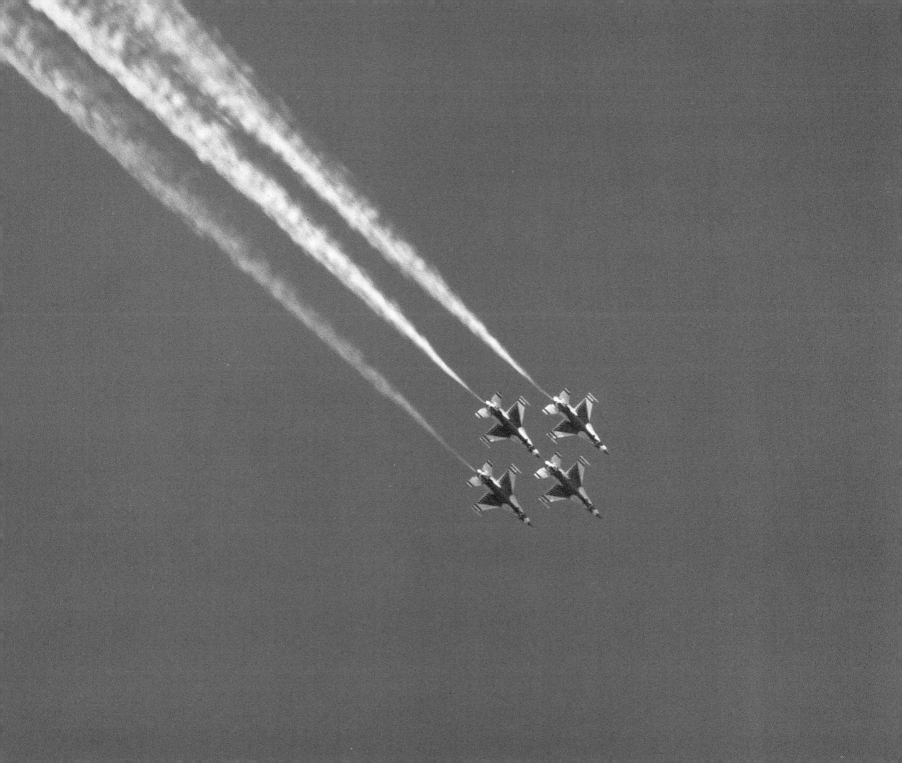

ONE

The Thunderbird Tradition

The red, white, and blue F-16 Fighting Falcon shakes the rooftops, and spectators clap their hands over their ears as the plane zooms by 300 feet overhead.

It is traveling at just under the speed of sound. Captain Pat Corrigan, 32, of Kokomo, Indiana, is at the controls.

Corrigan brings up the nose abruptly to begin a long, steep climb. Five g's of gravity flatten him against the seat.

At 6,000 feet, while still climbing, he kicks the sleek warbird into a tight vertical roll. Higher and higher he goes, the aircraft spinning like a top.

Corrigan flips on the smoke generator. A long, white spiral marks his trail as the plane becomes a silvery speck and then disappears from view.

Captain Corrigan is a Thunderbird, one of a team of six highly trained and experienced pilots that make up the Air Force's crack aerial demonstration squadron.

Since they first dazzled audiences in 1953, the Thunderbirds have performed in all fifty states and forty-six foreign countries. They have logged approximately 2,700 performances for nearly 200 million people.

Some of the maneuvers can take your breath away. The bomb burst and crossover is one. Four aircraft, flying in a diamond formation, suddenly pull up into a steep climb, trailing white smoke as they go. The four smoke plumes form a giant column in the sky.

Then the four planes swoop backward, each looping in a different direction. A fifth plane climbs through the center of the column, executing a series of spirals as it climbs.

Thunderbirds fly in famed diamond formation.

Spectators tilt back their heads and watch in awe. Thousands of cameras click.

The four pilots continue to loop, flattening out as they reach low altitude. Then they streak back toward the same fixed point above the runway, each zooming in from a different compass point.

Each pilot intends to reach that point at exactly the same time, allowing for just enough difference in altitude to avoid the most stupendous head-on crash of all time.

The crowd is wide-eyed. Some spectators cannot bear to watch.

The four planes get closer and closer. Then they whip by one another in a heart-stopping crisscross.

A wave of relief washes over the crowd. Cheers and applause ring out.

During their thirty-minute performance, the Thunderbirds offer thirty different maneuvers. Some of them involve four planes, others six. They range from the relatively simple diamond and arrow flyovers to intricate loops, turns, and rolls.

The mission of the Thunderbirds is to display the exceptional skills of the best Air Force pilots and to give their audiences an idea of what their planes can do.

Thunderbird officers normally serve a two-year tour of duty. All are handpicked, as are the enlisted men and women who are part of the Thunderbird team. These are the specialists and technicians who care for the planes.

All must compete against other applicants with outstanding records for selection. Once chosen, they are assigned to Thunderbird headquarters at Nellis Air Force Base near Las Vegas, Nevada. There they undergo months of rigorous training.

Each year, many hundreds of thousands of people get their first exposure to the U.S. Air Force through Thunderbird air shows. In the case of teenage boys and girls, an aerial performance can trigger a visit to a local Air Force recruiting office. As one observer put it, the Thunderbirds are "a flying recruiting poster."

In scores of foreign countries where they have flown, the Thunderbirds play a different role. There they give evidence of America's aerial might.

Both in foreign lands and in front of audiences in this country, the Thunderbirds are recog-

Thunderbirds are perfectly aligned in this six-plane maneuver.

nized as being the best at what they do. They are Air Force pride in action.

The Thunderbirds are one of several aerial demonstration squadrons active in American skies. The U.S. Navy offers the Blue Angels. A six-plane team, the Blue Angels began flying in 1946.

The Canadian Air Force boasts the Snowbirds, a nine-jet aerobatic team that frequently demonstrates its skills for American audiences. At New York's Coney Island on July 4, 1985, the Snowbirds performed for more than one million spectators.

There are also European demonstration squadrons. There are the Red Arrows of Great Britain's Royal Air Force, and teams in France, Italy, and West Germany.

Aerobatics, the art of performing stunts in an airplane, goes back to aviation's earliest days. In August, 1913, Lieutenant Peter Bestrov, a Russian airman, guided his aircraft through a closed curve on a vertical plane, a maneuver the shape of a bicycle wheel—a loop.

No one had ever done that before. One month later, an American, Lincoln Beachey, also looped an airplane.

After the loopers came the stunt fliers, hundreds of them. In the years following World War I and into the 1920s, some of the many thousands of men who had been trained to fly in the Army Air Corps crisscrossed the country giving aerobatic exhibitions in country towns and rural areas.

This was a time before airplanes were equipped with radios or other navigation aids. A pilot often got to where he was going by peering over the side of the plane and following railroad tracks.

At sundown or when bad weather threatened, he would put the plane down in any handy field. He would often shelter his plane behind a farmer's barn. Out of this practice came the term "barnstormer," used to describe stunt fliers of the day.

When the Air Force Thunderbirds stage their aerial demonstrations, they draw from a repertoire that includes loops and dives, rolls and spins, and other maneuvers similar to those the barnstormers once featured. But there the similarity ends.

Wheels down, Thunderbird F-16s approach for a landing.

The Thunderbirds are not stunt pilots. They never use the word "stunt" in describing what they do.

They're not daredevils. Every demonstration follows a carefully prepared script. Every maneuver is planned to the split second. Nothing is ever left to chance.

Safety and precision have keynoted the Thunderbird operation since 1953. That year, at Luke Air Force Base near Phoenix, Arizona, the Air Force's first demonstration squadron was formed.

The first Thunderbird pilots were chosen from among the trainees at the Air Force Advanced Flight Training School, which was based at Luke Field. Major Dick Catledge was named the team's first leader.

For its plane, the team selected the F-84 Thunderjet, an aircraft that had carved out an impressive record during the Korean War (which ended in 1953). The F-84 had flown more missions and dropped more bombs than any other fighter-bomber.

To convert the plane for use in aerial demonstrations, the guns were removed and the gun ports plugged.

Red, white, and blue scallops were painted on the nose, vertical tail, and wing-tip fuel tanks. Thirteen blue stars of different sizes were also painted on the tail. As a reminder of where the aircraft were based, the word LUKE was stenciled on both sides of the fuselage beneath the canopy.

Now all the team needed was a name. During June, 1953, a contest was held at Luke Field to find a name. "Thunderbirds" was the winning entry.

The choice was influenced, at least in part, by the Indian folklore of the southwestern United States, where Luke Air Force Base was located. From Mexico as far north as Alaska, the Thunderbird was well known in Indian folklore, common to such tribes as the Arapaho, Kiowa, Cheyenne, Comanche, Sioux, and Algonquian.

To many Indian nations, the Thunderbird held the same rank as the Sun God or Earthmaker. The Thunderbird produced thunder by the beating of its wings. It flashed bolts of lightning from its mouth or eyes. It was the Thunderbird that caused the rain to fall.

Accounts of what the bird looked like vary

somewhat from tribe to tribe. To some, the Thunderbird resembled a huge hawk or eagle. In southwestern United States, crude cave drawings and burnt outlines on leather have been found that depict the bird being red, white, and blue, colors commonly used by Indians of the area.

Some tribes believed the Thunderbird controlled the forces that saw good triumph over evil and light overcome darkness. It was the Thunderbird alone that could grant victory in war.

It is not hard to understand why the name "Thunderbirds" was chosen by the Air Force for its aerial demonstration team. Like the Thunderbird of legend, the Air Force Thunderbirds have the sky as their home. They flash through the air with the speed and brilliance

Flag decals blazoned on plane fuselages indicate foreign countries visited by Thunderbirds.

of lightning. They roar with a thunderous sound. And their mission—peace and goodwill—is in keeping with the age-old Thunderbird tradition.

TWO

A Dream Comes True

When Lloyd Newton—later to be nicknamed "Fig"—was born in Ridgeland, South Carolina, he was an unlikely candidate to be a Thunderbird pilot. For one thing, he was black, and black fighter pilots weren't even permitted to fly in combat with the U.S. Air Force until 1943, the year Lloyd was born.

Lloyd was raised on a ten-acre cattle farm, the fourth of seven children. About the only thing he knew about military aircraft was that once in a while fighter planes from a nearby Marine Corps air base would fly over the Newton farm.

Yet young Lloyd cherished a dream of being a pilot. When he was eighteen years old, and getting ready to graduate from high school, he talked to an Air Force recruiter and thought about enlisting.

"Go to college first," one of his teachers told him. "Then, after college, if you still want to join the Air Force, you can."

Lloyd followed that advice. After high school, he entered Tennessee State University in Nashville. He majored in mechanical engineering at first, then switched to the school's aviation education program.

Lloyd was also a member of the Air Force's Reserve Officers' Training Corps, the ROTC. That meant that while he was studying he was also earning a commission as a second-lieutenant in the Air Force.

After graduating from college and becoming a commissioned Air Force officer, Lloyd began jet flight training at Williams Air Force Base near Mesa, Arizona. "Off I went," he said, "proud and scared."

The war in Vietnam was raging at the time.

Thunderbirds fly in tight delta formation.

After he graduated from basic flight school, Lloyd received combat crew training at George Air Force Base, near Victorville, California. Then he was sent to Vietnam. "It was April, 1968," he recalls. "Things were hot and heavy there then." During his tour of duty in Vietnam, he flew 269 combat missions in the F-4 Phantom II, the Air Force's top fighter of the period.

Later, Lloyd, after having been promoted to the rank of captain, served four years at Clark Air Force Base in the Philippine Islands. At Clark, he was an F-4 flight leader.

"To lead a flight of four Phantoms around wasn't an easy task," he once told *Ebony* magazine. "It meant being responsible for eight lives and 12 million dollars worth of airplanes, a lot of responsibility for a young captain."

In 1972, while still in the Philippines, Lloyd sent in an application for a flying job with the Thunderbirds.

At the time, he wasn't wholly aware of how difficult it is to become a member of the Thunderbird team. In the first thirty-two years of the group's existence, only 158 officers managed to join the Thunderbird ranks.

Thunderbird officers usually serve for two years. They are then assigned to other Air Force duties.

Instead of training an entire new team every two years, two to four new officers come into the program each November. This makes for a smooth changeover from one team to the next.

To fill the vacancies, applications are accepted from pilots throughout the Air Force. And the applications pour in.

Each applicant must have at least 1,000 hours of flying time in jet fighters or jet trainers. He must have been commissioned as an Air Force officer for a period of not more than ten years. For the job of Commander/Leader, a minimum of 2,500 hours of jet-fighter or jet-trainer time is required.

The selection process lasts about four months. All of the applications are reviewed by the Thunderbird officers. Performance reports and recommendations from each applicant's superiors are evaluated.

For every spot open on the Thunderbird team, four semifinalists are chosen. The semifinalists travel to several show sites to meet the team and get an insider's look at the Thunderbird operation.

The semifinalists also travel to Nellis Air Force Base to be interviewed. There they fly in two-ship formations. Each pilot's performance is carefully evaluated by a third pilot in a chase aircraft.

The semifinalists undergo a very strict physical examination. They are interviewed by a board of senior officers and the commander of the Tactical Fighter Weapons Center at Nellis.

Finalists for each spot are selected. There are more interviews and more formation flying. A detailed profile of each candidate develops.

The Thunderbird pilots and senior officers make their recommendations. These are sent to the Commander of the Tactical Air Command, who makes the final decision.

White-uniformed Thunderbird pilots pose with special guests before a demonstration at Hanscom Air Force Base near Boston, Massachusetts.

Captain Lloyd "Fig" Newton

Captain Lloyd Newton went through the selection process, not once, but three times. The first time he applied, he finished as a semifinalist. The following year, he just missed as a finalist.

Then in 1974, on his third try, Newton heard the good news. The Thunderbird's Commander/Leader called him and said, "Congratulations. You've been elected for the Thunderbirds."

To Captain Newton, it was a dream come true. "All of us want to be the best in what we do," he said. "Well, from a flying point of view, the Thunderbirds are it."

Captain Newton was assigned to Thunderbird headquarters at Nellis Air Force Base for training in aerial demonstration flying.

In his first year with the Thunderbirds, Captain Newton did not actually fly with the team during demonstrations, but served as the team's narrator. During demonstrations, he was the public-address announcer, imparting background information about the team and explaining the various maneuvers.

Slot man's view as planes prepare for an arrowhead pass.

The next year, 1976, he took over as the No. 4 pilot, flying the slot plane in the diamond formation (see diagram). In the diamond formation, there are four planes. The No. 1 plane is the lead aircraft. The No. 2 and No. 3 planes, which fly side by side, are the wing aircraft. The No. 4 plane, the slot plane, flies in between the two wing aircraft.

DEEP DIAMOND

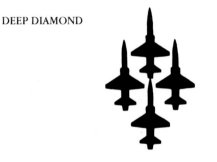

Captain Newton flew with the Thunderbirds again in 1978. In June, 1978, after having been assigned to another post, he was asked to come back and fill in for a pilot who was ill. He was very happy to return.

In the years that followed his service with the Thunderbirds, Captain Newton saw duty with the Legislative Liaison Office of the Secretary of the Air Force in Washington, D.C. In 1982, he served in Korea. By 1985, he had been advanced to the rank of Air Force colonel and was on assignment at the Pentagon in Washington.

Colonel Newton looked back fondly at his experience with the Thunderbirds. It wasn't merely because of the excitement and challenges the Thunderbirds offered him as a pilot. He also enjoyed the opportunity he had to speak to young people during appearances at schools and question-and-answer sessions following demonstrations.

"It gave me a chance to tell young people about the Air Force," he says, "about the opportunity one has to learn to fly and serve his or her country.

"But more than that, it gave me a chance to talk to young people about whatever goals they might have.

"When I was a kid, I always thought that my goal—to become a pilot—was out of reach. Well, I accomplished my goal. So I used to tell kids, 'If I was able to reach my goal, you can reach yours, too.' "

THREE

The Team

Each of the Thunderbird officers has a very specific job to do. Most of these assignments date to the Thunderbirds' earliest days. In 1953, when the first Thunderbird pilots were developing their aerial maneuvers and the sequence in which they were to be presented, they introduced the 3-and-1 formation. It is used to this day.

A lead aircraft and the two aircraft assigned to wing positions race down the runway closely followed by a fourth plane. Once the four planes are airborne, the trailing aircraft eases its way into the opening—the slot—between the wing aircraft. Thus is formed the diamond, the formation for which the Thunderbirds are now famous.

The diamond gives the Thunderbirds their basic assignments: leader, right wing, left wing, and slot.

During that first year, a fifth plane, a "spare" aircraft, took off before the diamond. The pilot's assignment was to scan the sky for aircraft that might have accidentally strayed into the demonstration area and also conduct a last-minute check of weather conditions.

The aircraft was also meant to serve as a backup. Had any one of the four other planes encountered a mechanical problem and been taken out of service, the fifth plane would have been called upon to fill in.

As the first season unfolded, the spare plane never had to be used as a performing aircraft. Thanks to the splendid maintenance they received, the four diamond aircraft performed flawlessly.

Someone then suggested using the fifth plane as part of the show. The fifth plane began taking off after the diamond and the pilot worked out a routine of his own that he performed. Of course, each of his maneuvers was timed to

blend with those of the diamond.

For example, when the solo pilot took off, and the attention of the crowd was focused on the departing aircraft, the four diamond planes would suddenly come hurtling over the heads of the spectators from behind. The screams of the startled onlookers all but drowned out the roar of the engine.

Later, the Thunderbirds added a second solo. Today, the two solos sometimes perform together; other times, singly. And still other times, they join the diamond aircraft to create five- or six-plane formations. Because of their triangular shape (see diagram), these are called delta formations. (Delta, which is the fourth letter of the Greek alphabet, has the shape of an equal-sided triangle.) Six-plane formations

SIX-SHIP DELTA

Diamond formation consists of lead plane, two wing aircraft, and slot man.

Six-plane formations are the most difficult the Thunderbirds fly.

are the most difficult that the Thunderbirds fly.

To spectators it may appear that the solo pilots are operating on their own. Not at all. They enter and exit the various maneuvers at speeds and altitudes that have been carefully determined in advance.

And the solo pilots, like the other pilots, are under the control of the Commander/Leader from the time their planes lift into the air until they are back on the ground again. He gives

No. 1 pilot, Commander/Leader Lieutenant Colonel Larry Stellmon.

them the commands to begin each maneuver, telling them the precise moment they are to roll or loop.

Today, the six Thunderbird pilots are designated as follows:

Thunderbird 1 — Commander/Leader
Thunderbird 2 — Left Wing
Thunderbird 3 — Right Wing
Thunderbird 4 — Slot
Thunderbird 5 — Lead Solo
Thunderbird 6 — Opposing Solo

Besides these six, there are five other officers who are members of the Thunderbird team. They are:

Thunderbird 7 — Logistics Officer
Thunderbird 8 — Narrator
Thunderbird 9 — Executive Officer
Thunderbird 10 — Maintenance Officer
Thunderbird 11 — Public Affairs Officer

The team's logistics officer is the squadron's deputy maintenance officer and also the safety observer. He watches each show from the ground and evaluates each pilot's performance. He also supervises the production of a videotape of the demonstration. The videotape is screened

F-16s on the ground

and discussed in a meeting with the pilots following the show.

Like the Thunderbird pilots numbered from 1 through 6, the logistics officer flies to the show site in an F-16. But his is a reserve aircraft, meant to be used should any of the other F-16s encounter serious mechanical problems and have to be removed from service.

The show's narrator is the public-address announcer during the show. He gives background information about the pilots and their aircraft. He explains each maneuver as it takes place.

That is only part of the narrator's job, however. He flies to the demonstration site in a two-seat T-38 Talon, arriving a few hours before the other Thunderbird pilots in their F-16s. The narrator is accompanied by the T-38's crew chief, the man responsible for the plane's maintenance. The two men get everything in final readiness for the demonstration.

The team's executive officer is the second in command, a deputy to the Commander/ Leader. Often he does not travel with the team, remaining at squadron headquarters at Nellis.

The maintenance officer is in charge of the

Red, white, and blue communications trailer is command post during air show.

repair and upkeep of all of the aircraft. The public affairs officer handles the team's relations with television, radio, and the press.

The Thunderbird pilots are supported by a group of slightly more than one hundred specialists and technicians (see Chapter Five). These are enlisted men and women, or non-

commissioned officers—noncoms or NCOs, for short. Their duties include everything from photography to airframe repair, from corrosion control to engine maintenance.

About fifty members of the support team travel to the show site aboard a huge Lockheed C-141 Starlifter. The others remain at Nellis. (The executive officer, maintenance officer, and public affairs officer also travel to the site in the C-141.) A four-engine jet, the Starlifter also carries spare parts and support equipment.

"We're a self-contained operation," says a Thunderbird spokesperson. "We travel just like a circus. Everything we need goes with us."

Maintenance personnel travel to demonstration sites in this C-141 Starlifter.

FOUR

Getting Trained

Nellis Air Force Base in the Nevada desert, eight miles north and east of Las Vegas, has been the Thunderbird "nest" since 1956. It is at or near Nellis where the pilots and support personnel live. Nellis is where they rest between assignments. Nellis is where pilots are trained.

Named to honor 1st Lieutenant William H. Nellis, a World War II fighter pilot killed in Europe in 1944, Nellis Air Force Base is blessed with one day after another of blue skies and bright sunshine—perfect flying weather.

What makes Nellis notable, however, is its size. Together with its ranges, areas where the Thunderbirds are able to fly without interfer-

ence from other aircraft, Nellis blankets 3,012,298 acres, or about 4,700 square miles. That's a chunk of land almost as big as the state of Connecticut.

Despite their enormous size, the ranges are largely uninhabited. Insects, lizards, snakes, and small burrowing animals are about the only permanent residents.

Each November when the demonstration season ends, the Thunderbird team returns to Nellis. They say their good-byes to the pilots who are leaving the team for other assignments. They welcome the newcomers. Almost immediately training begins for the season that is to open the following March.

The purpose of the training season is to teach the new pilots the techniques of aerial demonstration flying. At the same time, the veteran pilots, the holdovers from the previous season, have to get used to flying with the new men.

The training season involves thirty sorties, or missions. New pilots, however, fly at least twice that number. Before beginning instruction in the F-16, each new pilot flies several sorties in a T-38 Talon, a two-seat trainer. He occupies the back seat. In the front seat is an

instructor pilot from the 64th Weapons Squadron, which is based at Nellis.

The new pilot is taught advanced aircraft handling techniques. The instruction he gets makes him a better pilot and gives his confidence a boost.

In his first sessions in the F-16, the new pilot is schooled in level flight and wide turns at low altitudes. He has to learn to overcome any tendency he might have to look down at the ground. Instead, he must learn to concentrate on whatever maneuver is being flown.

The new pilot's first formal training exercise is a formation takeoff involving only two aircraft. As he masters simple maneuvers, he advances to ones that are more complex.

He practices inverted flight and inverted turns. He flies some figure 8s. Whenever the new pilot flies, a chase plane is in the sky to observe him.

The new pilot tries some *chandelles*. These are climbing turns in which speed is reduced to a point wherein the plane ends up using only its momentum to climb higher.

Not until his seventh sortie is the new pilot permitted to try a diamond takeoff. Five-ship maneuvers begin with the eighteenth sortie.

Not only must the new pilot learn to operate his plane while flying within a hairsbreadth of other planes, he must learn to do so while coping with tremendous g (gravity) forces.

A "g" is the force or pull of earth's gravity on the body at sea level. When a pilot pulls a plane out of a dive, he or she feels an extra weightlike force. If the force is twice the standard amount, it is rated at two g's. This means that the pilot's body must support twice as much force as it does normally.

Thunderbird pilots, in steep dives, experience as much as 5 g's or even 6 g's. Each pilot wears a pressurized suit—called a g-suit—to offset the pulling strains of gravity, which can cause a loss of consciousness in a matter of seconds.

Each Thunderbird pilot is assigned a particular role—Commander/Leader, right wing or left wing, lead solo or opposing solo, or slot. "Every pilot has the skill to fly any one of the positions," says Captain Dave Commons, who flew right wing for the team in 1985. "The assignment you're given is based upon whatever position happens to be open.

Thunderbirds fly over Hoover Dam, not far from Nellis Air Force Base.

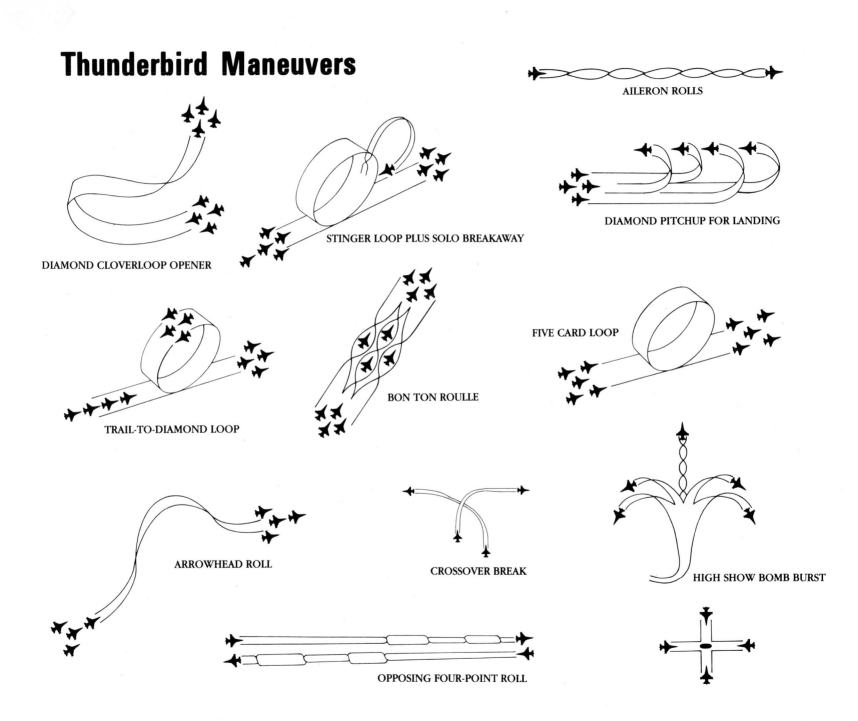

Thunderbird Maneuvers

AILERON ROLLS

DIAMOND CLOVERLOOP OPENER

STINGER LOOP PLUS SOLO BREAKAWAY

DIAMOND PITCHUP FOR LANDING

TRAIL-TO-DIAMOND LOOP

BON TON ROULLE

FIVE CARD LOOP

ARROWHEAD ROLL

CROSSOVER BREAK

HIGH SHOW BOMB BURST

OPPOSING FOUR-POINT ROLL

"But once you go through the training season flying a particular position, you fly that position for the entire year. The only way you can change from one position to another is to go through the whole training season."

At the same time the diamond formation pilots are sharpening their skills, any new solo pilot is also being trained. The new solo pilot practices at moderate altitude before attempting manuevers at the relatively low altitude at which shows are flown.

Once the new pilots have mastered all of the basic maneuvers, they begin practicing the timing between the solo pilots and the diamond. These sorties are videotaped. The tapes are screened after each performance and each maneuver is discussed.

By the time he is ready to fly his first official aerial demonstration, the new pilot is highly skilled. He already has the experience of a pilot who has flown anywhere from forty to fifty shows.

The Thunderbirds' concern for safety and

Underside view of Thunderbird F-16s in formation.

excellence is never ending. For instance, every takeoff is executed in a diamond formation, just as if it were being performed for a big audience.

When the Thunderbirds travel from one city to another, they always fly in precise formation. And when they arrive at a show site, they execute a few maneuvers before landing. They're not merely advertising their arrival; they're familiarizing themselves with their new surroundings.

When the team is at Nellis Air Force Base between shows, the pilots fly midweek practice drills.

Every time they fly, the Thunderbirds shoot for precision to the inch. A pilot who is a second late in executing a maneuver had better have a good explanation of what caused the delay.

A demonstration pilot can't afford to be anything less than precise. There is no margin for error when you're a Thunderbird.

Flying in delta formation, the Thunderbirds head for another show.

FIVE

The Support Team

Showing off the Air-Force's frontline fighters and the precision flying skills of their pilots is only one aspect of the Thunderbird's mission. The team also seeks to showcase the highly trained enlisted personnel responsible for the care and maintenance of the aircraft.

The Thunderbird support team is made up of 110 specialists and technicians. They are trained in a wide variety of different fields. Some are responsible for the aircraft electrical systems or the fuel systems. Others maintain the aircraft power plants, the engines, and still others, the avionics systems, that is, the aircraft electronics.

The support team also includes videotape technicians and weapons specialists, and administrative and public affairs personnel.

Approximately fifty members of the support team travel from Nellis Air Force Base to the show site aboard the Thunderbirds' support plane, the C-141 Starlifter. With them go all of their support equipment, including spare parts and an assortment of trailers from which the F-16s are serviced.

Suppose the engine of an F-16 has to be removed. Maintenance personnel wheel the engine-removal trailer up to the aircraft. The trailer contains the lifting gear and other equipment that enables them to do the job.

Crew chiefs are the most important of the support personnel. There are eight of them, one for each of the Thunderbirds' eight aircraft.

Each crew chief is responsible for the flight readiness of the plane to which he or she is assigned. Each has an assistant to help out.

Being assigned to a specific airplane gives the crew chief and the assistant a greater sense

Crew chief performs a preflight inspection.

Landing gear inspection is part of preflight check.

of pride in their work. If they were working on several different airplanes, they might not feel such pride. They work in a more dedicated fashion, and the aircraft benefits.

Sometimes a crew chief encounters a maintenance or repair problem that needs the attention of a specialist. He then calls upon one of the 100 or so technicians that make up the support team.

"You can't do it all on your own," says one

crew chief. "Keeping these planes in shape is very much a team effort."

To enlist in the Air Force, a boy or girl has to be at least seventeen years old and have earned a high school diploma. He or she must meet physical standards set by the Air Force and be of good character.

"We won't take anyone who has ever been

Crew chiefs and their assistants on parade before an air show.

arrested on drug charges or charged with driving while intoxicated," says an Air Force spokesperson. "The Air Force is a little picky."

Tests taken by the recruit help to indicate his or her field of interest. Some recruits are assigned to administration or management, others to electronics or telecommunications, and still others to aircraft maintenance. Of those assigned to maintenance, only a small handful gets to work with the Thunderbirds.

"Being with the Thunderbirds is a Special-Duty Assignment," explains Staff Sergeant Rodger (Dutch) Freiberger, 28, from Riverside, California, a crew chief with the Thunderbirds in 1985. "You have to apply for it, go through a selection process.

"You have to send the Thunderbirds what is called a 'package.' It consists of performance reports for the years that you've been in the Air Force. It also includes letters of recommendation from your superiors. And a photo.

"You mail it off. The Thunderbirds review the package. If they're interested, they send for you. They interview you and review your background and experience.

"If they like you, you then go through a 21-

day observation period. During that time, you meet everybody and see how the squadron operates. They get a chance to see what kind of work you can do.

"Then, after the 21 days, if they still like you, you're welcomed aboard; you're in."

At one time, the U.S. Air Force was as all-male as professional football. Not anymore. During 1985, of the 585,000 active members of the Air Force, 66,500, or about 11 percent, were women.

The Thunderbird support team has included several women. One was Technical Sergeant Cheryl Pascal, 27, a nine-year Air Force veteran. From California, Pascal was a maintenance specialist in aircraft systems—heating, air conditioning, pressurization, and oxygen systems. In Air Force slang, she was a "wrenchbender."

Besides her duties as a systems specialist, Pascal was also the assistant crew chief on the No. 1 Thunderbird plane, the Commander/Leader's F-16.

"I was always interested in airplanes," Pascal once recalled. "My dad was an aviation machinist in the Navy, a crew chief on the Grumman S-2 Tracker."

Pascal was the oldest in a family of three children, two girls and a boy. "Whenever my father asked us what we wanted to do on weekends, I always wanted to go to a local airfield and watch the planes take off.

"As I got older, I started thinking, 'I could work on planes; I know I could.'

"I didn't want to fly them or travel in them.

Cheryl Pascal

But I did enjoy watching them and working on them."

After high school and a year of college, Pascal enlisted in the Air Force. "I went through basic training and then they gave me my choice of jobs, and I chose the one I have now [systems specialist]. Then they sent me to technical school.

"After that I was assigned to my first base, McChord Air Force Base [near Tacoma, Washington]. There I got on-the-job training.

"That's what the Air Force is all about—you're always learning, always training. That's probably what I like the most about it."

Pascal says that during her early years in the Air Force she had no ambition to join the Thunderbirds. Then something happened to change her mind.

"I had just finished three years of duty at Clark Air Force Base in the Philippines, where I had worked on fighters, and had been transferred back to McChord. There I was stuck on big planes, four-engine C-130s and C-141s. To work on these planes, you have to climb up onto the center-wing area. And the components are bigger and heavier.

"One day the Thunderbirds came to my base to give a demonstration. I loved those pretty little jets. They seemed to call out to me. I went out and walked all around them.

"When the crew chiefs came out, they told me I could volunteer for the Thunderbirds. So I did. I put in a package. My application was approved and I was 'hired on.'"

At the time she joined the Thunderbird team, Pascal was the only woman in what had long been thought of as a man's field. "It was a struggle at the beginning," she recalled. "I had to stand on my own two feet. In fact, I had to work twice as hard to prove myself. You've got to do it. It's the only way.

"Once you're there and they get used to you, they accept you. But now and then I still have to do something extra to make a couple of guys see that I'm there because I deserve it. I'm not getting any special favors. I've fought for it."

In the first months she spent as an assistant crew chief, Pascal learned the basics of inspecting the aircraft, cleaning and servicing it, and performing general maintenance.

Technical Sergeant John Dvorachek was the

Crew chief checks a cockpit of an F-16 before a Thunderbird show.

plane's crew chief. "John is it as far as that aircraft is concerned," Pascal said. "Anything that happens to that plane, John should know about it.

"Having an assistant helps him to concentrate on the bigger problems. If I can do the little things, it helps him out."

The day of a show can be frantic for Pascal and her co-workers. "Say we're at Nellis," she once recalled. "We get up early, before dawn. We get the airplanes ready for the flight to the show site.

"We get on the Starlifter and fly to the site. If we arrive before the F-16s, we set up the landing area for the planes.

"While the pilots are getting briefed for the show, we get the jets ready. We inspect them, look them over. We check for leaks, check the tires. We check to see that the engine hasn't taken any rocks into the intake area.

"We clean up the airplanes. Wipe them down. We prepare the cockpit for the pilot.

"Then we help to launch the planes for the show. We watch the show, then recover the aircraft.

"Afterward, we go to the crowd line for autographs. We stand beside the pilot and simply hand him folders that he signs.

"We help him answer questions. If the crowd gets a little pushy, we help control them.

"The next morning, we're off to another site. Then the routine begins all over again."

SIX

Milestones

On June 1, 1953, the aerial demonstration team that soon was to become known as the Thunderbirds gave its first performance. Nellis Air Force Base was the scene. The team presented fifteen minutes of breathtaking maneuvers, drawing oohs and aahs from the audience of Air Force personnel and their families.

Several weeks later, on July 19, at a "Frontier Days" celebration in Cheyenne, Wyoming, the Thunderbirds gave their first performance for a nonmilitary audience.

By August, 1953, the team had flown twenty-six shows. At the Dayton (Ohio) Aircraft Show in September of that year, the Thunderbirds attracted a throng of 400,000, the first indication of the enormous popularity the team was to achieve.

By the end of the first season, the team had flown fifty shows. Nowadays, the team flies eighty to ninety shows each season.

In January and February, 1954, the Thunderbirds made their first foreign tour, traveling to Central America and South America. A show in Havana, Cuba, drew half a million spectators. When the team visited Mexico City, the audience topped the one-million mark.

Early in 1955, the Thunderbirds made a decision to switch from the F-84 Thunderjet to a more modern version of the plane. While the F-84 was a jet aircraft, it was not supersonic, that is, it could not exceed Mach 1, the speed of sound. (Sound waves travel at from 600 to 790 miles per hour through the air, depending on temperature and altitude.)

The F-84 Thunderjet was a straight-wing fighter; the wings were not swept back. The new version, however, called the F-84F Thunderstreak, boasted swept-back wings.

The Thunderstreak was the first of the team's aircraft to be equipped with smoke tanks. Now, at the flick of a switch, each plane could be made to trail a long plume of white smoke. This made it easier for spectators to follow the intricate maneuvers the aircraft traced in the sky. The smoke also boosted the dramatic appeal of each performance.

With the introduction of the F-84F, the show expanded from fifteen to nineteen minutes and its excitement level was heightened by the elimination of dead spots. Whenever the diamond streaked past the spectators and then out of their view, one or both of the solo pilots would dart in from the other direction. At least one Thunderbird was always on stage.

In 1956, the Thunderbirds began flying the sweptwing F-100 Super Sabre, the first Air Force jet capable of going beyond the speed of sound while in level flight or climbing. (Earlier jets could attain supersonic speeds only by diving.)

During this period, one or the other of the solo pilots would make a supersonic pass, a maneuver that never failed to delight the crowd. But eventually the Federal Aviation Authority banned supersonic flight at air shows. The loud sonic booms created whenever the sound barrier was pierced had drawn complaints from those living near air bases. Sometimes the sound

waves cracked window glass or caused other physical damage. All Thunderbird demonstrations are performed at subsonic speeds today.

A 40-day tour during 1959 took the team to the Far East for the first time. They performed for more than three million people in Taiwan, Korea, Japan, Okinawa, and the Philippines. For this feat, which involved more than 24,000 miles of travel, the Thunderbirds received a high honor—the Mackay Trophy. It is given each year for outstanding achievement in the world of aviation.

A record 2,053,000 spectators turned out in Rio de Janeiro, Brazil, in November, 1961, to watch the Thunderbirds. That still ranks as the biggest crowd in Thunderbird history. The two million people who watched them perform in Chicago in 1959 set an attendance record for a performance in the United States.

In May, 1963, the Thunderbirds made their first European tour. Shows were presented in Portugal, France, England, Luxembourg, Germany, Italy, and Spain. Time after time as the team moved from one country to the next, inflight refueling was relied upon.

The Thunderbirds continued to fly the F-100 until 1968. However, for a brief period in 1964, the team switched to the F-105 Thunderchief. A big, heavy plane, about twice the weight of the F-84 Thunderjet, the Thunderchief was sometimes referred to as the "lead sled" by Air Force pilots of the day.

Six shows were flown in the F-105s. Then, on May 9, 1964, Captain Eugene Devlin, flying in a group of three planes at 500 feet, put his aircraft into a climb, when suddenly it exploded. The Air Force immediately grounded the team.

Instead of cancelling the 1964 schedule, the team went back to the F-100 Super Sabre. The Thunderbirds closed out 1964 with fifty-nine demonstration shows in the F-100.

One of the team's busiest years was 1965, when the Thunderbirds gave a record 121 demonstrations. One of these, at Waukegan, Illinois, marked the team's 1,000th performance.

The season of 1967 was highlighted by another European tour. At its conclusion, the Thunderbirds made a nonstop flight from Paris to the U.S. Air Force Academy in Colorado Springs, Colorado, a distance of 7,000 miles.

F-100 Super Sabre was the plane flown by the Thunderbirds beginning in 1956.

Seven times the F-100s were refueled in the air.

A demonstration at Nellis Air Force Base on November 30, 1968, rang down the curtain on the F-100 era. It had lasted twelve years. No aircraft served the Thunderbirds for a longer period. In those twelve years, the Thunderbirds gave 1,111 shows at home and abroad.

During the years from 1969 through 1973, the Thunderbirds flew what had become the workhorse plane of the Air Force, the F-4 Phantom II. A two-seat, twin-engine aircraft, the F-4 was used by three branches of the armed services during the Vietnam War. Air Force F-4s flew both day and night missions, pounding North Vietnamese troop positions. The aircraft was used by the Navy as an all-weather fighter, and by the Marines as a fighter-bomber and interceptor.

The first Thunderbird demonstration using the F-4 was given on June 4, 1969, at the Air Force Academy. President Richard Nixon, enjoying his first year in office, was one of the spectators.

In a salute to the more than 1,000 American servicemen who were being held prisoner by the North Vietnamese, the Thunderbirds added a missing man formation to their routine. As the aircraft approached the audience flying in the diamond formation, Thunderbird 3, the left wing, would suddenly pull up. The other three planes continued the pass. "You watch them go by and you can't help but get chills," said one spectator.

A 30-day tour of Europe in 1971 took the Thunderbirds to Spain, Denmark, Germany, Belgium, Italy, and France. At Bourget Airport in Paris, the team performed before 800,000 spectators one day, and 1,500,000 the next.

Through the years, Thunderbird performances had attracted upward of one million people on a number of occasions. But at least one performance was noteworthy for the smallness of the audience. At Clear, Alaska, in 1969, the Thunderbirds took to the air to perform for a gathering of 39 individuals. It was the smallest "crowd" to ever watch the team, and the only one in which the spectators were outnumbered by the Thunderbird team itself and their support crew.

In 1973, the Thunderbirds performed before more than 12 million spectators in the United

Thunderbird T-38s pass Golden Gate Bridge and San Francisco Bay.

States and Latin America, a record number for one year. Their final show that season, performed on November 10 in New Orleans, Louisiana, was also the final performance for the F-4 Phantom II.

During 1973, Arab oil-producing nations had put a ban on oil petroleum exports to the United States. In response to the fuel crisis which gripped the nation, the Thunderbirds gave up their F-4 Phantom IIs in favor of the fuel-efficient T-38 Talons.

The T-38 was not a fighter but a training plane. It was, in fact, the world's first supersonic trainer.

There were some drawbacks to the T-38. Its small size made it more difficult for spectators to pick it up when it was high in the sky. And since the aircraft was not capable of being fueled while in flight, it meant that there would be no shows in Europe, nor in any location that required long-distance travel.

But the T-38 offered certain advantages, besides fuel economy. It was a marvelously maneuverable aircraft, able to make very tight turns. Some maneuvers that could not be flown efficiently in the F-4 seemed tailor-made for the

T-38. Also, the plane didn't require as big a maintenance crew as the F-4.

The T-38 helped to enrich the Thunderbird tradition. In 1976, when the nation was celebrating its 200th birthday, the tails of the Thunderbird T-38s were adorned with the official bicentennial symbol.

When the National Air and Space Museum in Washington, D.C., opened in 1976, the Thunderbirds were there. A show at the Mountain Home Air Force Base not far from Boise, Idaho, on May 8, 1976, marked the Thunderbirds' 2,000th official performance.

In total, Thunderbird T-38s participated in 598 demonstrations in forty-six states, Canada, Puerto Rico, and the Dominican Republic.

During 1976, T-38 Talons wore nation's official bicentennial emblem.

SEVEN

The Fighting Falcon

The Thunderbirds were plagued with tragedy in 1981 and 1982.

During the summer of 1981, an accident at Hill Air Force Base near Ogden, Utah, took the life of one of the members of the team. Then in September of that year, the team's Commander/Leader was killed during a takeoff at the Cleveland airport.

In December, back at Nellis, the saddened team members began to prepare for the season of 1982. It was to be the last year for the T-38s.

The Talons were scheduled to be replaced by the F-16 Fighting Falcon, the Air Force's top-of-the-line supersonic fighter.

On Monday morning, January 18, the four diamond aircraft soared above the Nevada desert, practicing a line-abreast loop. It was not a particularly difficult maneuver. It looked like a backflip from a diving board.

In executing it, the T-38s were to race along, wing tip to wing tip, about 100 feet above the ground. They then were to zoom up to 2,500 feet, loop backward into a dive, pulling out when they got back to 100 feet.

The pilots had performed the maneuver many times. At the beginning, everything went as planned. The four planes sped along, wing tip to wing tip. They climbed to 2,500 feet, then swooped back toward the ground.

But this time they did not pull out. The lead plane went plunging into the ground. The three others followed within a tenth of a second.

The four planes exploded in a ball of flame that one witness said looked like a napalm explosion of the type he had seen in Vietnam during the war. All four pilots were killed on impact.

Investigators probed through the wreckage in an attempt to find clues as to what caused the terrible accident. They eventually were able to establish that a loose bolt had gotten stuck in the horizontal tail surface of the lead jet.

With its stabilizer jammed, the lead plane could not pull out of its dive. The three other pilots followed the leader. CRASHING IN FORMATION declared a headline in a news magazine.

The eighty shows the Thunderbirds had scheduled for 1982 were cancelled. But the Air Force had no thought of turning its back on the Thunderbird program. Plans were put in motion immediately for training new pilots in new aircraft.

THE TIME:
April 2, 1983

THE PLACE:
Nellis Air Force Base
near Las Vegas, Nevada

THE EVENT:
The opening of the Thunderbirds'
thirty-first season

It is comeback day for the Thunderbirds, their first performance after an absence of eighteen months. The whole crew is brand-new. So are the aircraft. The T-38s have been replaced by combat-ready F-16 Fighting Falcons.

Captain John Bostick, a solo pilot on the new team, had known the four pilots who had been killed eighteen months before. He was asked whether his memory of the accident bothered him. He answered: "If your best friend is killed in a car, it doesn't mean you'll never drive a car again. You go on flying in a very professional and safe manner."

Safety is one of the leading features of the F-16. The plane has, in fact, earned the best safety record of any single-engine fighter in Air Force history.

The F-16 boasts a power plant that can deliver 15,000 pounds of thrust. This increases to 25,000 pounds when the afterburner is switched on. (The afterburner is a device that burns the engine's exhaust fumes, giving the aircraft an abrupt boost in power.)

The steep twisting climb, described at the beginning of this book, couldn't have been performed in a T-38. The plane didn't have enough power. But the F-16 performs the

White-painted Thunderbirds contrast sharply with Nevada landscape.

Thunder F-16s parked on taxi strip, canopies raised, await call to action.

breathtaking climb using only 60 percent of power available to it.

When it comes to speed, the F-16 is capable of something beyond Mach 2 (twice the speed of sound) at 35,000 feet.

During a show, the jets cruise at well beneath top speed. The unused speed, which is there should a pilot need it, makes for increased safety.

Besides its more-than-needed store of speed and power, the F-16 is one of the most maneuverable aircraft ever ordered by the Air Force.

52

F-16 FIGHTING FALCON

Manufacturer:	General Dynamics; Fort Worth, Texas
First flight:	December 8, 1976
Acquired by Thunderbirds:	June 10, 1982
Length:	49½ feet
Wingspan:	32¾ feet
Height of vertical tail:	16 feet
Design weight:	22,500 pounds
Maximum takeoff weight:	35,400 pounds
Speed	
Maximum Level:	Mach 2 +
Cruising:	650 mph
Takeoff:	135 mph
Landing:	125 mph
Ceiling:	Above 50,000 feet
Rate of climb:	More than 30,000 feet per minute
Roll rate	
gear retracted:	324 degrees per second
gear extended:	167 degrees per second
Propulsion system:	One Pratt & Whitney F-100-PW-200 afterburning turbofan engine; 25,000-pound thrust class

Thunderbirds in line-abreast formation.

On combat duty, F-16s wear camouflage gray.

The control stick is of the force-feedback type. Suppose the pilot wants to bank sharply to the left. He simply moves the stick hard in that direction. Soft pressure on the stick makes for a gentle turn.

The F-16 cockpit is built to hold the pilot comfortably in his seat, even when the pressure gets as high as 8 g's.

The seat, along with its bubble-shaped cover, or canopy, offers the pilot visibility in every direction, a full 360-degree viewing area. During a show, this means always being able to see your wingman or the man in the slot. In combat, it could mean no enemy is going to come sneaking up behind you.

The Thunderbird F-16s can be turned into combat planes within 72 hours. It means installing the avionics—the aviation electronics—that fighter planes require and their weapons systems.

This includes such air-to-air weapons as the M61 20-mm multibarrel cannon and Side-winder heat-seeking missiles. As for air-to-ground munitions, the F-16 can handle up to 15,000

pounds of rockets and bombs. Making a combat plane out of the F-16 would also mean repainting the aircraft in camouflage gray.

On the Thunderbirds' comeback day, April 2, 1983, the F-16s were ablaze with their red, white, and blue color scheme. The Thunderbird design in dark blue had been painted on the underside of the fuselage of each aircraft.

The audience included hundreds of fighter pilots who were in training at Nellis Air Force Base. The show crammed thirty maneuvers into a program that lasted a half hour. It drew thunderous applause from the pilots seated in the stands as well as from the civilian spectators.

To the Thunderbirds, the show was no comeback. It was a fresh start, the beginning of an era meant to carry the fame and glory of the Thunderbirds to new heights.

EIGHT
On Stage

"Good afternoon, ladies and gentlemen. The United States Air Force Thunderbirds are extremely pleased to be with you today."

That's how the Thunderbirds' narrator opens a show. Local dignitaries are introduced. So are the pilots, wearing their white flight suits.

Now they stand at attention on the flight line. Their planes are parked wing tip to wing tip behind them.

As many as a quarter-of-a-million spectators are likely to be on hand, perhaps even more. Early arrivals watched the preshow activity.

The planes were towed into place on the flight line. Then they were fueled and their engines warmed up. Crew chiefs and the as-

Captain Jake Thorn handles narrator's chores.

sistant crew chiefs inspected the planes. There was one last polishing of the gleaming red, white, and blue striping.

Other noncomissioned officers set up and tested the microphone and loudspeakers to be used by the show's narrator. They greeted the "DVs"—distinguished visitors—and helped arrange for their seating. They assisted TV cameramen and still photographers in getting into position.

It is now only minutes before the planes lift into the air. "The Thunderbirds are named after one of the most famous legends in American Indian folklore," the narrator explains. "The magestic Thunderbird was believed to cause thunder and lightning, to grant success in war, to conquer evil."

As the theme from *Superman* blares forth, the pilots climb into their planes. The crowd presses against the restraining ropes and barriers.

The stage is set. It's time to fly.

The narrator says: "Let's watch and listen as the engines of the Thunderbird F-16s come to life."

The engines begin a high-pitched whine. The

Crowd gathers for a show at Hanscom Air Force Base, Boston, Massachusetts.

planes turn and taxi slowly in a single line toward the airport runway. Spectators in the front rows cover their ears with their hands. The smell of burned jet fuel fills the air.

"The Thunderbird pilots are now on the runway to your right," the narrator says, "and will soon run up their engines for takeoff." He identifies the pilots one-by-one and explains the role of each.

Before the show, Thunderbird is towed from its hangar to the flight line.

The No. 1 aircraft then streaks down the runway. It is followed in an instant by the other three. The narrator says: "As the four planes climb sharply from the runway, the slot plane moves quickly into the slot position to form the famous Thunderbird diamond.

"Following the diamond will be the lead solo. As he clears the runway, he will show you the slow speed rolling ability capability of these aircraft.

"The second solo will take off and execute an immediate pull-up to demonstrate the F-16's impressive power and rapid acceleration."

The six planes are now in the sky. Quickly they group together in an arrowhead formation, turn and head back for the flight line.

The narrator says: "And now, with their distinctive red, white, and blue markings, trailing plumes of white smoke, ladies and gentlemen, here they are, your United States Air Force Thunderbirds!"

A wave of anticipation engulfs the huge crowd. Every pair of eyes turns upward. The theme music from *Chariots of Fire* is blotted out by the earsplitting roar from the six jets.

The thirty-minute demonstration usually con-

Air show souvenir stands feature Thunderbird balloons.

sists of some thirty different maneuvers. There are the diamond roll and arrowhead roll. There are the diamond cloverleaf and the high show bomb burst and crossover. By midshow, the crowd is already limp.

One of the favorite maneuvers is also one of the most difficult—the trail-to-diamond roll. In this, spectators are given a clear demonstration of the raw power and great maneuverability of the F-16.

TRAIL-TO-DIAMOND ROLL

The four aircraft enter the maneuver at 300 feet. Each is flying a few feet above the next, like steps in a staircase.

"Nose up!" the leader calls out. The four aircraft pull up sharply. At the order, "Rolling left," the formation, still climbing and now at about 2,500 feet, makes a 25-degree roll to the left.

Now the four aircraft are at about the same level. The leader stays in the lead. The No. 2 aircraft moves to his left. The No. 3 plane goes to the right. No. 4 fills the slot so that the planes form the diamond.

To get into the slot in time, No. 4 has to call on extra power. The other aircraft are racing along at 400 mph. No. 4 has to exceed 500 mph for a split second.

When No. 4 is in the slot, he notifies the others by saying, "Four is in." The leader responds with the command, "Into float." Instantly the diamond turns upside down, the four planes rolling together at 2,500 feet.

They slow to just over 200 mph until the leader calls out, "Back in with pull." The jets come right-side up, then dive toward the ground at 20 degrees off the horizon.

At the command, "Power up, smoke off; ready, *now!*" the team makes a left turn past the crowd at 300 feet and gets into position for the next maneuver.

Every show demands not only precise execution but also proper placement. What good does it do to execute a thrilling maneuver if it occurs a mile away from the audience?

To assure that each maneuver occurs at the

Each maneuver at each show is carefully timed from the ground.

After each maneuver, the leader will call the safety observer to ask whether the No. 1 plane was targeted on show center.

"Was it right or left?" he'll ask.

"About 200 feet to the right," the safety officer might answer. "So move it back to the left."

After the demonstration has ended and the planes have landed and been parked, the spectators are invited to come forward and meet the pilots. For as long as their schedule permits, the pilots, assisted by their crew chiefs, answer questions, pose for photos, and give autographs.

Thunderbird pilot obliges with an autograph.

right spot, the Commander/Leader keeps in radio contact with the team's safety observer. The safety observer watches the show from the communications trailer, parked near the flight line.

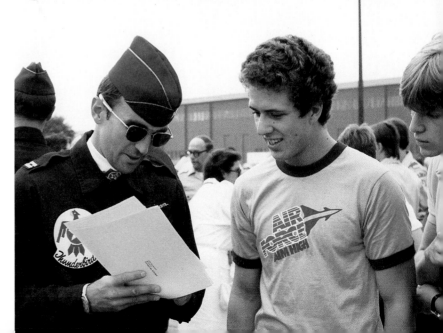

It is usually late afternoon by the time the last question has been answered and the last autograph signed. The aircraft are sheltered in a hangar for the night.

There's more to do for the pilots, however. They must be debriefed. They meet and discuss every detail of the demonstration they've just completed.

The No. 7 pilot, who serves as the squadron's safety observer, conducts the debriefing. He has watched the show carefully and given each maneuver a grade. He has also supervised the timing and videotaping of every maneuver.

During the debriefing, the safety observer plays the videotape for the pilots. Each maneuver is examined. The safety observer makes comments about each one, explaining why he thought it was good or telling why he downgraded it.

"And we make comments among ourselves," says Captain Dave Commons. "We'll ask things like, 'What did you do there?'

"We're always striving for the perfect air show," says Commons. "Realistically, that's not possible, because of the human factor. But that's what we're always trying to achieve."

Glossary

AEROBATICS — Stunts performed by an airplane.

AFTERBURNER — A device within a jet engine that serves to burn the engine exhaust fumes, giving the aircraft a quick increase in power.

AILERON — The movable edge of the wing that controls the plane's roll.

AVIONICS — The science of electronic devices in aviation.

COMMISSIONED OFFICER — An officer who holds the rank of second lieutenant or above.

CREW CHIEF — The noncommissioned officer responsible for the flight readiness of a Thunderbird plane.

DELTA — A six-plane formation, triangular in shape.

G — Symbol used to rate the weightlike forces of gravity.

G-SUIT — The pressurized suit worn by a pilot to offset the pulling strains of gravity.

LINE ABREAST — Any maneuver in which aircraft fly wing tip to wing tip.

LOOP — A maneuver in which an aircraft traces a closed curve on a vertical plane.

MACH — The ratio of the speed of an aircraft to the speed of sound. An aircraft traveling at Mach 1 is traveling at the speed of sound; at Mach 2, twice the speed of sound, etc.

NCO — Abbreviation for noncommissioned officer.

NONCOM — Short for noncommissioned officer.

NONCOMMISSIONED OFFICER — An enlisted member of the armed forces.

RESERVE OFFICERS' TRAINING CORPS (ROTC) — A body of students at college or university that is given training toward becoming officers in the Air Force or other branches of the armed services.

SLOT PLANE — In the diamond formation, the No. 4 plane, positioned to the rear and in between the two wing aircraft.

SORTIE — The flight of an aircraft on a specific operation or mission.

SQUADRON — A unit of four or more aircraft of the same type.

STABILIZER — The horizontal tail surface of an aircraft.

SUBSONIC — Less than the speed of sound waves through the air. *See* Supersonic.

SUPERSONIC — Greater than the speed of sound waves through the air. (Sound waves travel at from 600 to 790 miles an hour, depending on temperature and altitude.)

WING — An Air Force unit of several squadrons.

Index

797.5
Sul

Sullivan, George
The Thunderbirds

DATE DUE			
NOV 1			
APR 20			

143   87

MEDIALOG
Alexandria, Ky 41001